Contents

Page

List of Illustrations

Chapter 1

Introduction

We may be likened to two scorpions in a bottle, each capable of killing the other, but only at the risk of his own life.

- J. Robert Oppenheimer, 1953

Ideological differences between the US and its greatest antagonist, the Soviet Union, have been the underpinnings to the majority of foreign politics since the end of World War II. In the 50 years following, the global community lived under both the blanket and shadow of nuclear arms as the two superpowers kept their arsenals and the concept of nuclear deterrence at the center of their respective national security strategies. The United States' foremost objective was singular in scope: to prevent the Soviet Union from attacking the United States and its allies and protect US interests abroad. To this purpose the country designed and built a diverse and survivable nuclear force coupled with an extremely effective conventional capability against a singular adversary.[1] Primarily designed around the US nuclear triad and the North Atlantic Treaty Organization (NATO) alliance, this strategy was relatively successful against Soviet communist expansion.

However, as stated as early as 2001 and reiterated in the 2006 Quadrennial Defense Review (QDR), large state actors are no longer the sole primary threat. While they remain of interest, current challenges include newly emerging powers, hostile regimes, and non-state/non-governmental actors who may not respond in-kind to the traditional concepts of deterrence.[2]

This paper will argue that though the utility of the Cold War-era nuclear deterrent strategy will likely remain effective towards those adversaries who respond to the threat of coercive punishment, policy makers will be challenged to develop more adaptive, flexible and uniquely tailored deterrent strategies to counter future national security threats. While US policy recognizes the need to deter all forms of weapons of mass destruction (WMD), this paper focuses primarily on the nuclear element.

Understanding Deterrence

What is *nuclear deterrence* and how does nuclear deterrent strategy work? Before explaining the what, how and why of nuclear deterrence, certain general distinctions should first be made. Although Carl von Clausewitz argued war is simply an extension of politics, the use of the military arm of national power throughout history has been for states to persuade others to do their bidding.[3] As witnessed by the numerous wars throughout human history, this was often derived through the direct application of brute force. However, successful persuasion has also occurred through a somewhat indirect means using a threat of the application of force.

When referring to the concept of coercion, there are two forms: compellence and deterrence. *Compellence* is the coercive strategy that persuades the adversary to act for fear of the consequences if they do not.[4] It is often considered the more difficult of the two forms of coercion to achieve as it requires the adversary to do something against his will, an act that is overtly submissive to the coercer's demands. The best example of compellence (i.e., coercive diplomacy) occurred during the Cuban missile crisis in 1962. A peaceful outcome was achieved when President Kennedy chose to use a diplomatic strategy using positive inducements (promising not to invade Cuba and removing Jupiter

2

missiles from Turkey) along with punitive threats (the US naval blockade of Cuba and the perceived willingness to escalate to war). This "carrot and stick" approach induced Soviet Premier Kruschev to remove the missiles.[5] Conversely, an example in which attempts at compelling an adversary failed is the Allied strategic bombing offensive against Germany during the Second World War. The targeting of industry and civilians did not produce the intended outcome of demands for capitulation by the German citizenry.

According to strategist Lawrence Freedman, the concept of deterrence, simply put, is about "inducing inaction."[6] The *American Heritage Dictionary*, defines deter as, "to prevent or discourage the occurrence of an action, as by means of fear or doubt."[7] Joint Publication 1-02 defines deterrence as "the prevention from action by fear of the consequences. Deterrence is a state of mind brought about by the existence of a credible threat of unacceptable counteraction."[8] In other words, it is the form of coercion that uses the threat of retaliation—punishment—to influence an adversary's behavior to not act for fear of the consequences. It encourages maintaining the status quo by inhibiting a decision-maker from a particular act with compliance measured by their non-activity. As Yale theorist Patrick Morgan defined it:

> Deterrence involves manipulating someone's behavior by threatening him with harm. The behavior of concern to the deterrer is an attack; hence, deterrence involves the *threat to use force in response* as a way of preventing the first use of force by someone else.[9] (emphasis added)

Morgan goes on to suggest there are conceptually two kinds of strategic deterrence, immediate and general. *Immediate* deterrence occurs when two adversaries are preparing for direct conflict; one side is considering an attack while the second threatens retaliation.[10] Returning again to the Cuban missile crisis example, when the Soviet Union's plans to install nuclear-tipped ballistic missiles on Cuba were revealed, President Kennedy's direct response is an illustration of immediate deterrence. *General* deterrence, on the other hand, occurs when overt threats between rivals are avoided, yet a status quo is preserved by each maintaining the capability to retaliate.[11] This is much more typical of foreign politics and probably most commonly recognized as the Cold War. It would also be reasonable to suggest that states practice general deterrence in hopes of avoiding immediate deterrence.[12]

Obviously, historic cases of immediate deterrence are more readily apparent, and studies to determine their successes or failures are easier to distinguish, unlike general deterrence where it is much more difficult to determine relative outcome. This is because accurate data for case studies of general deterrence may be more difficult to obtain. The aversion of war is not automatically an example of a success in general deterrent strategy if the attacker never intended to attack, nor would it be considered a failure if the defender did not attempt to deter the attacker.[13] Therefore, one could argue it is difficult to determine whether general deterrence was successful between the US and the Soviet Union after 1970.[14]

Associated with the concepts of immediate and general deterrence are the ideas of central and extended deterrence. *Central* deterrence refers to discouraging attacks upon one's homeland, e.g. the US dissuading Soviet attack on its native soil; whereas in *extended* deterrence, the deterree broadens its deterrent umbrella to include its allies.[15] The US providing regional protection to allies both in the North Atlantic Treaty Organization (NATO) and Asia is one example.

Finally, the overarching concept of deterrence may be distinguished between denial and punishment. Deterrence by *denial* attempts to convince an adversary that military and political objectives cannot be accomplished without great cost.[16] Since it typically targets the adversary's military forces, this is often referred as a *countermilitary* strategy.[17] For example, the US blockade along the Taiwan Straits during the Korean conflict. Deterrence by *punishment* attempts to dissuade an adversary by threatening what it values, in general, civilian industrial or economic centers. Thus, it is referred to as a *countervalue* strategy.[18]

In the end, US strategic deterrent efforts work to affect adversaries in three ways: 1) deny benefits; 2) impose unacceptable costs; and 3) encourage restraint.[19] The difficulties lay in discovering and executing unique but effective deterrent strategies across a broad range of adversaries. But success is not simply determined by the adversary perceiving the costs of a given course of action outweighing the benefits. Instead, adversaries must also weigh their actions against the consequences of *inaction*. For example, in 1950, People's Republic of China Chairman Mao Zedong committed the People's Liberation Army into the Korean conflict despite multiple assurances that UN forces would not enter Chinese territory. Mao's actions were likely due to his fear of US threats to Chinese sovereignty since UN ground forces reached the Yalu River north of the 38th parallel while US Navy's 7th Fleet was simultaneously blockading the Taiwan Straits to protect Taiwan from the communist Chinese. Therefore, deterrence can still fail even when the adversary believes the cost outweighs the benefits of a particular course of action if the cost of inaction is greater still.[20]

The Proliferation of Nuclear Weapons

At the end of World War II, the United States was the sole proprietor of nuclear arms until 1949 when the Soviet Union successfully tested its own nuclear weapon. By the early 1960s, two more countries (the United Kingdom in 1951 and France in 1960), both US allies, developed and tested their nuclear weapons. [21] Less than five years later, China became the fifth nuclear power with support from the Soviet Union, but by 1968, the Treaty on the Non-Proliferation of Nuclear Weapons, otherwise referred to as the Non-Proliferation Treaty (NPT), attempted to prohibit the further spread of nuclear weapons. [22] According to its provisions, the five nuclear weapons signatories (US, USSR, UK, France, and China) agreed not to help other states acquire or build nuclear weapons; and non-nuclear weapons signatories, of which there are over 180, agreed not to acquire or develop nuclear weapons. [23] However, there are three states that have not signed the NPT and maintain a nuclear arsenal: India, Israel, and most recently, Pakistan. Figure 1 highlights those states that own or purportedly own nuclear weapons. India first tested a device in the mid-1970s, and Pakistan conducted its own successful test in 1998. [24] Israel, however, maintains a policy of ambiguity, though a secret nuclear weapons program was disclosed in the mid-1980s. [25]

Despite the provisions of the NPT and the relative success since its inception, it is likely the future will see more states declaring themselves *nuclear powers*. Iran and North Korea are most notable; however, countries such as Japan, Turkey, South Korea, Egypt, Saudi Arabia and Taiwan should be observed for their future capability and intent. [26]

Notes

[1] Department of Defense, *National Defense Strategy*, June 2008, 11.

[2] Department of Defense, *Quadrennial Defense Review Report*, February 2006, 32.

[3] Robert A. Pape, *Bombing to Win: Air Power and Coercion in War*, (Ithaca, NY: Cornell University Press, 1996), 1.

[4] Lawrence Freedman, *Deterrence*, (Cambridge: Polity Press, 2004), 26.

[5] Alexander George, *Forceful Persuasion: Coercive Diplomacy as an Alternative to War*, (Washington DC: United States Institute of Peace, 1991).

[6] Freedman, 110.

[7] *The American Heritage® Dictionary of the English Language, Fourth Edition.* "deter", Houghton Mifflin Company, 2004 http://dictionary.reference.com/browse/deter.

[8] Joint Publication (JP) 1-02, *DoD Dictionary of Military and Associated Terms*, 12 April 2001, 162.

[9] Patrick M. Morgan, *Deterrence: A Conceptual Analysis*, 2d ed, (Beverly Hills, CA: Sage Publications, 1983), 11.

[10] Ibid., 27-49.

[11] Ibid.

[12] Ibid., 43.

[13] Kenneth Watman et al., *US Regional Deterrence Strategies*, RAND Report MR-490-A/AF (Santa Monica CA: RAND, 1995), 14.

[14] Ibid., 13-15.

[15] Ibid., 15.

[16] Ibid., 16.

[17] Ibid.

[18] Ibid.

Notes

[19] *Deterrence Operations Joint Operating Concept v2.0*, December 2006, 5.
[20] Ibid., 20-21.
[21] Olav Njølstad, "The Development and Proliferation of Nuclear Weapons", *The Norwegian Nobel Institute* (http://nobelprize.org/educational_games/peace/nuclear_weapons/readmore.html).
[22] Ibid.
[23] Ibid.
[24] Ibid.
[25] Ibid.
[26] Maj Gen Donald Alston, "The Air Force Nuclear Enterprise" (video teleconference lecture, Air War College, Maxwell AFB, AL, 9 September 2008).

Chapter 2

Will Nuclear Deterrence Work Today?

Nuclear deterrence doesn't work outside of the Russian-U.S. context;
Saddam Hussein showed that.
                                                    - Gen Charles Horner

The Cold War Role of Nuclear Weapons

The term *deterrence* has often been associated with the general conduct among nation-states. Yet since the end of World War II and the advent of nuclear weapons, it has evolved to achieve a distinctive connotation that has been synonymous with the concept of *nuclear* deterrence.[1] In military parlance, deterrence emphasizes the potential consequences after an attack—how the retaliatory response would not only increase the cost to the attacker, but also reduce benefits. Since deterrent strategies rely on the threat to use force, the deterrer's earnestness to *make good* on those threats if the deterrent strategy fails is a key factor in one's credibility.[2] Thus, the deterred must appreciate both the willingness and capability of the deterrer. During the Cold War, the negative consequences of a Soviet conquest of Western Europe was incalculable, hence the use of nuclear weapons in an extended deterrent role for the defense of Western Europe was generally regarded as credible.[3]

Among the many reasons nuclear deterrence was arguably successful during this period was the posited inability of the attacker to defend against retaliation. US nuclear strategy focused on its ability to effectively respond following an enemy's surprise attack. Investing in a two-pronged approach demonstrated the willingness of the United States to commit to this strategy. First, strategic planners designed an infrastructure to

9

assure US nuclear capability by ensuring the force would be launched before it was struck by the enemy. This ability to provide immediate response requires a highly-tuned command and control and an early warning capability. Second was the survival of a retaliatory force of credible size following such an attack. The ability to withstand an attack requires the retaliatory force be given a degree of protection through both diversity and dispersion.[4] Thus, the creation of a nuclear triad to project capability was designed. Hundreds of nuclear-tipped land- and sea-based ballistic missiles and manned bombers were able to deliver thousands of weapons, thereby demonstrating US capability. Land-based Intercontinental Ballistic Missiles (ICBM) provide a long-range first-strike capability. Though they are the most vulnerable of the three legs to the nuclear triad, they can be launched quickly and, once aloft, are difficult to intercept. Submarine-Launched Ballistic Missiles (SLBM) are substantially more survivable and, therefore, provide a retaliatory second-strike capability. Their slightly shorter range requires ballistic missile submarines to be closer to enemy shores; however, this also means the adversary has much less time to react between detection and impact. Finally, the strategic bomber force offers the greatest flexibility by offering both a first- and second-strike capability. By deploying forces to their *fail safe* locations, bombers also have a level of survivability, yet afford the greatest opportunity for recall.

Throughout the Cold War, US nuclear policy continually evolved against the Soviet threat and, therefore, modified its forces and targets to maintain credibility.[5] US doctrine migrated from the counterforce strategies of *massive retaliation* and *flexible response* in the 1950s and 1960s to the countervalue approach of *assured destruction*. Then, once the

Soviet Union acquired enough nuclear forces to achieve a second-strike capability in the late 1960s, the US modified its strategy labeled *mutually assured destruction.*[6]

A Changing Strategic Environment

For nearly 50 years, the United States approached its national security with a single focus: to deter the Soviet Union from attacking the United States and its allies. Likewise, the planning assumptions and calculus associated with deterring such a threat was based solely on understanding the dynamics and culture of this single enemy.[7] Today's deterrent environment is much more complex. With the collapse of the former Soviet Union and the resultant end to the Cold War, the United States' national security environment has evolved.[8] Within this environment are a changing Russia, emerging near-competitor nations such as China, hostile regimes such as Iran and North Korea, and transnational terrorism. But one thing is clear, their nature and motivations to either maintain or obtain weapons of mass destructive power offer a clear threat to the United States. The 2008 National Defense Strategy warns of today's deterrent challenges:

> In the contemporary strategic environment, the challenge is one of deterring or dissuading a range of potential adversaries from taking a variety of actions against the US and our allies and interests. These adversaries could be states or non-state actors; they could use nuclear, conventional, or unconventional weapons; and they could exploit terrorism, electronic, cyber and other forms of warfare. Economic interdependence and the growth of global communications further complicate the situation. Not only do they blur the types of threats, they also exacerbate sensitivity to the effects of attacks and in some cases make it more difficult to attribute or trace them.[9]

Consequently, this wider range of adversaries will increasingly employ military forces across the entire range of military operations, most notably in irregular warfare.

"US dominance in conventional warfare has given prospective adversaries, particularly

non-state actors and their state sponsors, strong motivation to adopt asymmetric methods

to counter our advantages."[10]

Notes

[1] Bernard Brodie, *Anatomy of Deterrence*, RAND Report RM-2218 (Santa Monica, CA: RAND, July 1958), 3.

[2] Abram M. Shulsky, *Deterrence Theory and Chinese Behavior*, RAND Report MR-1161-AF (Santa Monica, CA: RAND, 2000), 17.

[3] Ibid., 24.

[4] Brodie, *Anatomy of Deterrence*, 14-16.

[5] Amy F. Woolf, *Nuclear Weapons in US National Security Policy: Past, Present, and Prospects*, CRS Report RL34226 (Washington DC: Congressional Research Service, updated January 2008), 6.

[6] Robert Doughty, et al., *American Military History and the Evolution of Western Warfare*, (Boston, MA: Houghton Mifflin, 1996), 851-864.

[7] Department of Defense, *National Defense Strategy*, June 2008, 11.

[8] *National Security Strategy of the United States of America*, 2002, 13.

[9] Department of Defense, *National Defense Strategy*, June 2008, 11.

[10] *Ibid.*, 4.

Chapter 3

The Current Security Environment

We must always remember that it would be a fatal thing for the great free peoples to reduce themselves to impotence and leave the despotisms and barbarisms armed.

- President Theodore Roosevelt

The 2005 National Defense Strategy and its newest iteration in 2008 both recognize the challenges of the 21st century. As noted in the 2006 QDR, state actors no longer have a monopoly on weapons of mass destruction; tyrants and terrorists have no shortage of will and are trying to gain the capacity to possess their own WMD arsenal.[1] Though US strategic nuclear force structure has changed little since the end of the Cold War, the increasing number and differing types of players, coupled with differing concepts of nuclear strategy and their means of delivery, will make nuclear deterrence much more difficult.[2]

One of the difficulties inherent with owning nuclear weapons is whether they would be utilized as a response to anything less than a direct, massive attack against the US, and if so, convincing an enemy of that resolve. Recent articles allude to the current administration's concerns over obstacles to nuclear deterrent strategy.[3] Among these hurdles: its irrelevancy due to the lack of a serious enemy; opponents who cannot be stopped either due to religious fanaticism or, in the case of the North Korean president, someone who has an "erratic and sometimes tenuous grip on reality;" or that regional dynamics impact US deterrent influence.[4] Looking closer at these new threats, what are examples of the challenges to US deterrent strategy?

Russia

Russia will not soon become, if it ever becomes, a second copy of the United States or England - where liberal value have deep historic roots.

- Vladimir Putin

The Soviet Union of the Cold War era was a known ideological opponent in which hostility was mitigated with an emphasis on nuclear deterrence. Although military stability was not exclusively nuclear, the reliance on this component in any crisis between the superpowers caused both the US and Soviets to remain extraordinarily cautious as nuclear weapons existed in overwhelming numbers to allow for total annihilation.[5] However, today, the US administration and, subsequently, US strategy routinely look towards Russia as a country in transition that is unlikely to pose a military threat to the US or its allies in the same scale or intensity as its former self.[6] While this may be true, "images of Russian tanks rolling into Georgia were a reminder that nation-states and their militaries do still matter."[7]

The 2001 Nuclear Posture Review states Russia may not be an immediate threat, but:

> Russia's nuclear forces and programs, nevertheless, remain a concern. Russia faces many strategic problems around its periphery and its future course cannot be charted with certainty. US planning must take this into account. In the event that US relations with Russia significantly worsen in the future, the US may need to revise its nuclear force levels and posture.[8]

Russia's efforts to aggressively test and field new warheads and delivery systems remain an area of concern. Among the Russian efforts to modernize its nuclear forces include a maneuverable warhead, a new generation of RS-24 intercontinental ballistic missiles, a new submarine-launched ballistic missile, SS-NX-30 (Bulava), and a new, Borey-class ballistic missile nuclear submarine all scheduled to be fielded within the next five years.[9] One can argue that it is a reasonable expectation for a nation to modernize its military whenever it has the resources to do so. As demonstrated by its recent efforts, it appears Russia is not yet willing to relinquish its grip as a major nuclear power, but in perspective, Russia may just be looking to "dominate its 'near abroad'—not an ideologically driven campaign to dominate the globe."[10]

China, a Near-Peer Competitor

The art of war teaches us to rely not on the likelihood of the enemy's not coming, but on our own readiness to receive him; not on the chance of his not attacking, but rather on the fact that we have made our position unassailable.

- Sun Tzu

For approximately two hundred years, the world has been shaped by the west. Colonization by the French and British of the Asian and Australian continents, as well as the opening of trade with Japan by the United States helped to reinforce this concept. Yet recently, there has been a steady growth of power and influence in the east and the proliferation of nuclear capabilities is but one outcome. Beginning with China in the mid-1960s, the acquisition of nuclear capability in the eastern hemisphere has steadily risen; first with India, most recently with Pakistan, and always with the continued suspicion of North Korea.

Of the emerging powers, the United States looks towards China as the ascending state with the greatest potential for competition[11], and certainly as the rising regional hegemon in the east. The Chinese military has not yet had a reputation as a top-tier fighting force but is seen primarily as a tool to suppress internal political conflict. [12] As with all major nations, the Chinese have been working to both modernize and transform their forces. Although there is uncertainty in the true amount of Chinese defense expenditures, it is suspected that they have increased their spending by more than 10% per year since 1996, with heavy investments in asymmetric capabilities to include missile technology, cyber, space, and anti-satellite systems.[13] Their heavy emphasis on national security and corporate espionage has quickly reduced the technological advantage the US once enjoyed. China has effectively compressed 25 years of missile development into a few short months and nuclear weapons research into a few short years.[14]

China has always been perceived by the west to be exceptionally demure in its intentions. Whether this is due to a failure to appreciate cultural differences or miscommunication is not within the purview of this paper, yet it can be widely argued the United States has not been adept in interpreting Chinese perceptions or their idea of *rational thinking*. Herein lies the issue behind having a coherent nuclear deterrent strategy between the United States and China:

> ...deterrence theory has presumed a degree of rationality on each side in a conflict that encompasses at least the following capabilities: the ability to accurately evaluate the opponent's military strength, the ability to read the opponent's intentions, and the ability to accurately predict the effects of one's statements and actions on the perceptions and behavior of an opponent.[15]

Some describe the "Asian way of war as one of indirect attacks, avoiding frontal assaults meant to overpower an opponent."[16] While it may sound trite, it has been argued that the classical strategic writings of Sun Tzu and other eastern strategic philosophers truly offer a glimpse into what inspires and translates into China's strategic culture of subtlety and manipulation.[17] Alternatively, one can look at the method in which the Chinese try to influence their environment. While the western method of problem resolution is based on a direct, *cause and effect* approach, eastern societies would rather look to indirect methods and sometimes focus on second- or even third-order effects to deflect the opponent from a particular outcome. In other words, unlike western societies which seek a specific conclusion, eastern societies look to avoid a particular ending. Figure 2 illustrates this concept.

Figure 2: Deflecting Outcome via Indirect Influences

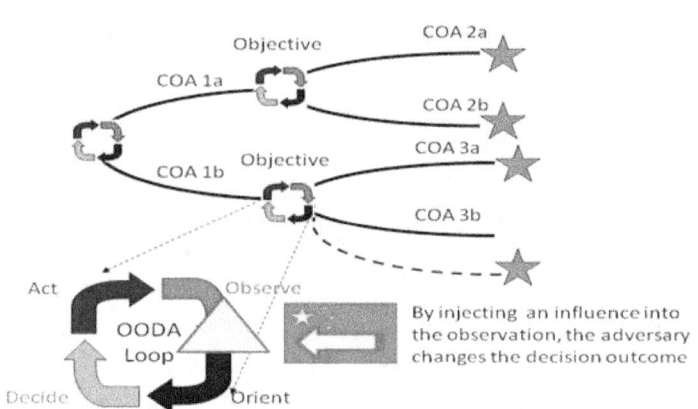

Source: Adapted from Col James Greer briefing on Chaos and Complexity: The Impact of the New Sciences on Military Operations, 3 Jan 03

It is likely China will want to translate its growing power into greater authority within the region.[18] Truth be told, however, no one outside of China truly has knowledge of its motivations or intent.[19] The fundamental precept in the western idea of nuclear deterrence is about dissuading the aggressor by weighing the consequences of their actions and appreciating the resultant retaliatory response as one that would be so unacceptable in costs it eliminates any hoped-for gains. In this regard, while neither country has ever established a *no first use* policy, both the United States and the Soviet Union invested extensively in early warning capabilities to assure prompt retaliation of a

17

first strike from the other side. Of note, however, is while China maintains a nuclear arsenal and a prompt, capable delivery system in its ballistic missile fleet, they currently do not have, nor have they ever emphasized, development in an early warning capability. Perplexing questions for US observers are: What are the Chinese trying to signal? How will this influence Chinese (and subsequently US) foreign policy?[20]

But looking from a more pragmatic perspective, should not US strategists rather ask, "What is the US trying to deter with respect to China?" and "Is it worthy of a threat of nuclear retaliation?" US nuclear deterrent strategy towards the Soviet Union was developed around the context of the US containment policy offered in NSC-68/4 and, therefore, it was Soviet expansion that was at its heart.[21] As RAND analyst Abram Shulsky fittingly points out:

> Since deterrence primarily relies on the threat of future harm, the deterrer's credibility is obviously a key factor in making deterrence work. Credibility may be determined by many factors; one of the most important is the importance to the deterrer of the stakes involved. In the Sino-US context, the importance of the stakes involved in many of the potential deterrence situations may not be so clear.[22]

The relationship between China and Taiwan is one of great contention and perhaps one of the few issues with stakes worthy enough to merit the costs of inflicting punishment. Yet even here, the US policy towards Taiwan is one which strongly supports its democracy but not one which demands independence. On the contrary, the US is committed to a *one China policy*. Among the policy's core principles is the US government's opposition to any unilateral moves by either China or Taiwan—especially by force—to change the status quo.[23] Therefore, while the US is willing to strategically accept Taiwan's incorporation into China, it is the manner in which change is achieved that is of interest to the US. Convincing China that the process vice the substance of reunification is substantial enough to incur the US' wrath may be too weak of a basis for US credibility.[24] Shulsky points to historic reference that successfully deterring China often required a high level of threat.[25] The Taiwan Strait crisis in 1954-1955 required both a US blockade and a threat to use nuclear weapons to convince Beijing to stop its hostile activity. Whether the US can afford to do so today is questionable. With China's own nuclear capability, would the US' extended deterrent policy be willing to trade Taipei, for say, Los Angeles?[26] What is not disputed is that any deterrent strategy will be more difficult to apply towards China than it was in the US-Soviet Cold War.[27]

One thing is clear, with respect to China, "a deterrence policy which discourages an opponent from employing some options but not others is incomplete and may not prevent a failure of deterrence. An opponent who is bent upon altering a given status quo may design around the viable aspects of the deterrence strategy that confronts him. That is, he may seek to formulate an option for challenging the status quo that takes advantage of loopholes, weaknesses, or uncertainties...."[28] China has always been adept at measuring its activity in a manner as to avoid strong response from its adversary. Shulsky refers to this as "salami tactics" where rather than grabbing the whole salami, the aggressor takes small slices, none of which is big enough to warrant a response by the defender, yet in the end, the aggressor winds up with the entire salami.[29] Based on this assessment, it would seem difficult to establish an effective Chinese nuclear deterrent strategy.

Regional/Hostile States

Israel must be wiped off the map. And God willing, with the force of God behind it, we shall soon experience a world without the United States and Zionism.

- Iranian President Ahmadinejad

Rogue states tend to threaten international order.[30] The 2002 National Security Strategy outlines the shared attributes of rogue states. Among them are their willingness to disregard international law, threaten their neighbors and wantonly violate international treaties; their determination to acquire weapons of mass destruction; and their sponsorship of terrorism around the globe.[31] Whereas in the Cold War when weapons of mass destruction were considered options of last resort, today's enemies seek them as weapons of choice and a means to intimidate or blackmail other states while simultaneously overcoming the conventional military superiority of the United States.[32] Deterrent strategist Bernard Brodie recognized in 1958 what a nuclear capability brings to the voice of an "inferior" nation:

> Prior to the nuclear age, a force which was clearly inferior to a rival's might or might not have some real deterrence value…Now that we are in a nuclear age, the potential deterrence value of an admittedly inferior force may be sharply greater that it has ever been before.[33]

Consider the possible motivations of owning a weapon of mass destruction, especially a nuclear weapon, from a regional adversary's perspective:

- To deter military threats or attacks by the US and others
- To redress its military inferiority
- To enhance national prestige and influence

- To shore up domestic political support
- To ensure survival of the regime.[34]

For example, tensions between Pakistan-India may likely remain below large-scale military action due to their respective nuclear capability. One Pakistani general was quoted as saying, "Suppose Pakistan had been non-nuclear in 2002. There might have been a war. If there's one lesson I've learned, it's that possession of a nuclear weapon has not been a bad idea."[35]

In addition to the general purposes listed, North Korea may also see their nuclear program as a means by which to engage in "parasitic extortionism" to obtain foreign aid.[36] Yet to the majority of rogue states, the primary motivation for owning a nuclear arsenal may likely be the survival of the regime. In a recent monologue of regional adversaries by David Ochmanek and Lowell Schwartz of RAND Corporation, they contend that due to a "deficit of legitimacy" in such regimes, "the survival of the regime is often synonymous with the personal survival of those at the top of the regime."[37] There is some truth to this idea. The United States has already demonstrated in both Afghanistan and Iraq its willingness to "decapitate" the national leadership from their respective country, which in the case of Iraq eventually led to Saddam Hussein's execution.

Now that the motivations for why regional states may wish to acquire nuclear weapons have been identified, what are their likely objectives in threatening their use? Three have evolved:

- To deter US intervention within a region. This may be the most plausible use. If US interests in the region are relatively weak, increased risks may cause second-thoughts on the part of its leaders.

21

- To intimidate US allies within the region. Coercing US allies or creating division among an alliance or coalition would minimize US influence throughout the region.
- To limit US objectives and ensure survival of the regime. From the perspective of an enemy, a retaliatory threat as a "last ditch" effort to survive is entirely plausible.[38]

If nuclear deterrence worked against the Soviet Union, would it also work against regional adversaries? Most likely, the answer is "no." Unlike conflict with the Soviet Union, there are too many asymmetries:

- Defeat equals end of the regime (where state survival typically means personal survival)
- Conventional forces cannot prevent military defeat
- Using nuclear weapons may change the balance of a military situation towards the adversary's favor.[39]

Consider the Iranian position. After the US coalition war with Iraq as well as Afghanistan, Iranians feel a sense of isolation (some call it "strategic loneliness") and believe the only way Iran can maintain its territory, prestige and political survival is through reliance on a nuclear capability. Among several factors in Iranian decision making, its foremost priority surrounds regime survival.[40]

Iran's government has been aggressive in anti-US rhetoric, yet while it has threatened its neighbors, it has not behaved in a careless or irrational manner.[41] Similar to China, assuming a nuclear-armed Iran, what activity would the US find necessary to deter that would risk a nuclear exchange? Certainly an overt, first-strike use against a US ally could be reason for use, but any deterrent strategy "based on rational actor assumptions necessitates a good understanding of the adversary. Cultural ignorance, inability to communicate, or gaps in knowledge on both sides will complicate the strategic situation."[42]

Of greatest concern is the potential of a nuclear-armed Iran providing its weapons or radioactive materials to non-state actors. While the likelihood is unknown, the more difficult question would be whether the regime could prevent *leaks* to terrorists. More probable is the concern that violent extremists may feel more emboldened to conduct more aggressive activity within the region assuming it feels protected by a nuclear-armed Iran.[43]

North Korea finds itself with a similar preoccupation of regime survival. Domestic instability has been a consistent problem for totalitarian and authoritarian regimes. Because these regimes teeter on the brink of domestic failure, any internal or external crises causes its leadership to quickly and energetically respond.[44] Often, this may cause its leadership to be willing to accept greater risk to ensure its survival. The failed economic strategy of North Korean presidents, Kim Il Sung and Kim Jong Il has caused an estimated 2-3 million of North Korea's population to starve to death during the 1990s,[45] yet the country continues to heavily invest in missile and nuclear technology.

It may be argued a totalitarian or authoritarian government will trump regime survival over the value of its citizens. As a result, deterring these regimes will be difficult, and *traditional* Cold War deterrence is likely to be an ineffective strategy. As stated in the 2002 National Security Strategy:

> In the Cold War, especially following the Cuban missile crisis, we faced a generally status quo, risk-averse adversary. Deterrence was an effective defense. But deterrence based only upon the threat of retaliation is less likely to work against leaders of rogue states more willing to take risks, gambling with lives of their people, and the wealth of their nations.[46]

This does not necessarily mean nuclear deterrence cannot work. For a punishment strategy to be effective, the US must threaten what the adversary values most. While it is likely a countervalue strategy will likely be ineffective, a counterforce strategy aimed at the political stability of the regime or perhaps a decapitating approach would be more apt to succeed.[47] The difficulty is for the US to find—but not cross—the tipping point between effective nuclear deterrence and spooking a rogue nation to overreact.

Transnational Terrorism

The gravest danger our Nation faces lies at the crossroads of radicalism and technology. Our enemies have openly declared that they are seeking weapons of mass destruction, and evidence indicates that they are doing so with determination.

- President George W. Bush

The growth of the nuclear industry as well as the proliferation of technology and materials has increased opportunities for terrorists to engage in some form of "nuclear action."[48] "Terrorism is violence for effect" and typically a campaign designed to inspire fear, choreographed to achieve maximum publicity.[49] In 1975, public policy expert Brian Jenkins expressed his view on concerns with the potential nuclear terrorist threat in a testimony before the Committee on Energy and Diminishing Materials of the California State Assembly. His observations argue:

- The primary attraction to terrorists going nuclear is not necessarily the mass casualty aspect, but rather that any terrorist act associated with "nuclear" automatically generates fear. Terrorists may try to take advantage of this fear without the risks or investments necessary to build and detonate a working bomb
- Drawing attention to themselves and their causes, creating alarm and perhaps gaining political leverage can be achieved using relatively unsophisticated actions demanding less skill and risk
- The large, well-organized terrorist groups which may have the resources to undertake the above actions may also be constrained from these acts for fear

of polluting their cause, alienating their constituency as well as provoking immediate reprisal[50]

It is doubtful Jenkins would have foreseen the kind of violent, transnational terrorism the world is dealing with today, though he was somewhat prescient in his conclusions when he admitted extremists with nihilistic ideologies may not be "constrained by fears of alienating world opinion."[51] Despite no clear evidence a terrorist organization has actually seized a weapon or assembled its own device, the Joint Operating Concept for Deterrence Operations (DO-JOC) published in 2006 recognizes the fact that non-state actors are now able to pose threats to US interests and are therefore an integral element when developing US strategy.[52] Among the challenges to deterrence:

- Determining the non-state actor decision-makers we seek to deter
- General uncertainty on non-state actor decision-maker's perception of benefits, costs, and consequences of restraint
- Non-state actors differ in susceptibility to efforts to credibly threaten imposition of costs
- Determining non-state actor value sets, goals/objectives, and means to achieve them
- In contrast to state actors, non-state actors do not have well-established means of communication.[53]

Just as the asymmetries between the US and regional adversaries limit success in the use of traditional deterrence, it is with these challenges in mind that the 2002 National Security Strategy succinctly states, "traditional concepts of deterrence will not work against a terrorist enemy whose avowed tactics are wanton destruction and the targeting of innocents."[54]

Notes

[1] Department of Defense, *Quadrennial Defense Review Report*, February 2006, 32.

[2] Glenn Buchan et al, *Future Roles of US Nuclear Forces*, RAND Report MR-1231-AF (Santa Monica, CA: RAND, 2003), xvi.

[3] Fawzia Sheikh, "Pentagon Lays Out Three Obstacles to Nuclear Deterrence—Space Challenge Also Cited," *Inside the Pentagon*, 17 July 2008.

[4] Ibid.

[5] Watman, et al, US Regional Deterrence Strategies, 7.

[6] Department of Defense, *Quadrennial Defense Review Report*, 2006, 28-29.

[7] Robert M. Gates, "A Balanced Strategy: Reprogramming the Pentagon for a New Age" *Foreign Affairs* 88, no. 1 (January/February 2009): http://www.foreignaffairs.org/ 20090101faessay88103/robert-m-gates/how-to-reprogram-the-pentagon.html.

[8] Nuclear Posture Review (Excerpts), submitted to Congress on 31 December 2001, *2001 Nuclear Posture Review Report*, 17.

[9] Guy Faulconbridge, "Russia Starts Production of New Ballistic Missiles," *NewsDaily*, 1 Dec 2008 (Reuters), http:\\www.newsdaily.com/stories/tre4b03qa-us-russia-missile/.

[10] Gates, "Balanced Strategy".

[11] Department of Defense, *Quadrennial Defense Review Report*, 2006, 29.

[12] Paul Bracken, *Fire in the East: The Rise of Asian Military Power and the Second Nuclear Age*, (New York, NY: HarperCollins Publishers, 1999), 74.

[13] *2008 National Defense Strategy*, 3.

[14] Bracken, *Fire in the East,* 68-69.

[15] Morgan, *Deterrence*, 207.

[16] Bracken, *Fire in the East*, 126-127.

[17] Ibid.

[18] Department of Defense, *Quadrennial Defense Review Report*, 2006, 29.

[19] Ibid.

[20] Bracken, *Fire in the East,* 55.

[21] Shulsky, *Deterrence Theory and Chinese Behavior*, 18-21.

[22] Ibid., ix.

[23] James A. Kelly, "Overview of US Policy Toward Taiwan," Testimony at a hearing on Taiwan, House International Relations Committee, Wash DC, 21 Apr 2004.

[24] Shulsky, *Deterrence Theory and Chinese Behavior*, 25.

[25] Ibid., 36.

[26] Douglas Paal and Dr. Nancy Bernkopf Tucker, interview by Andrea Koppel, "China and Taiwan: An American Tightrope," *Transcript of Great Decisions TV 2001*, (http://www.fpa.org/topics_info2414/topics_info_show.htm?doc_id=77090).

[27] Shulsky, *Deterrence Theory and Chinese Behavior,* viii.

[28] Ibid., 30-31.

[29] Ibid.

[30] Department of Defense, *2008 National Defense Strategy*, 3.

[31] *The National Security Strategy of the United States*, September 2002, 14.

[32] *Ibid.,* 15.

Notes

[33] Brodie, *The Anatomy of Deterrence*, 7-8.

[34] David Ochmanek & Lowell H. Schwartz, *Challenge of Nuclear Armed Regional Adversaries*, (Santa Monica, CA: RAND, 2008), 15.

[35] Ibid., 35.

[36] Andrew Scobell, North Korea's Strategic Intentions, (Carlisle Barracks, PA: Strategic Studies Institute, US Army War College, 2005), 18-29.

[37] Ibid., 15-16.

[38] Dean Wilkening & Kenneth Watman, *Nuclear Deterrence in a Regional Context*, RAND Report MR-500-A/AF (Santa Monica, CA: RAND Corp, 1995), 32-36.

[39] Ochmanek, *Challenge of Nuclear Armed Regional Adversaries,* 40.

[40] Judith S. Yaphe and Charles D. Lutes, *Reassessing the Implications of a Nuclear-Armed Iran*, McNair Paper 69, (Washington, DC: Institute for National Strategic Studies, NDU, 2005), 3-4.

[41] Ibid., 39.

[42] Ibid., 40.

[43] Ibid., 41.

[44] Watman, et al, *US Regional Deterrence Strategies*, 35.

[45] Ochmanek, *Challenge of Nuclear Armed Regional Adversaries,* 25.

[46] *The National Security Strategy of the United States*, Sep 2002, 15.

[47] Watman, et al, *US Regional Deterrence Strategies*, 72-73.

[48] Jenkins, Brian M., *Will Terrorists Go Nuclear?*, RAND Paper P-5541 (Santa Monica, CA: RAND Corp, 1975), 1.

[49] Ibid., 4-5.

[50] Ibid., 4-9.

[51] Ibid., 7.

[52] *Deterrence Operations Joint Operating Concept, v2.0*, Dec 2006, 18-19.

[53] Ibid.

[54] *The National Security Strategy of the United States*, Sep 2002, 15.

Chapter 4

The Effectiveness of Today's Strategic Deterrent Strategy

To be prepared for war is one of the most effectual means of preserving peace.
- George Washington

Are Nuclear Weapons Still Necessary?

Simply put, yes. The current Secretary of Defense, Robert M. Gates stated this pragmatic argument plainly, "[A]s long as others have nuclear weapons, we must maintain some level of these weapons ourselves: to deter potential adversaries and to reassure over two dozen allies and partners who rely on our nuclear umbrella for their security—making it unnecessary for them to develop their own."[1] The traditional role nuclear weapons are expected to play in the foreseeable US deterrent strategy is both viable and indispensible.

Ironically, nuclear weapons may now become the weapon du-jour of militarily *weak* countries. Once the *crown jewels* of technologically advanced powers, *leveling* technologies such as Global Positioning System navigation and ballistic missile technology have merged with the increased proliferation of nuclear weapons technology to allow emerging countries to obtain these weapons. Note that the most recent countries to obtain a nuclear capability—India, Pakistan, and perhaps North Korea—are not considered economic heavyweights. Of interest is the cost in acquiring these systems may, in whole, be cheaper than maintaining a conventional capability and is likely seen as an effective alternative to countering US conventional superiority.[2]

28

Internally, the US has shifted its national security objectives away from maintaining nuclear parity with a single adversary to one that protects itself from the broad range of external threats. Emerging from the Cold War, the President recognized the need to prepare the military for an era "of the unexpected and the unpredictable" and directed the military to transform its forces to confront these new threats.[3] United States Strategic Command, chartered with the mission to provide the nation with global deterrence capability, responded with the need for a more flexible, adaptive capacity and has replaced the traditional, rigid Single Integrated Operations Plan (SIOP) with one that has a more flexible approach analogous to current conventional target planning[4] to allow for a wider range of contingencies and adversaries.

But there are limits. Coercion based on the threat of retaliatory punishment is no panacea to deter all forms of aggression or conflict. Externally, the world is transforming. The capabilities and national objectives of old adversaries have changed since the Cold War and new global challenges include players who have differing sets of values and influences, and may not appreciate the *rules of the game* the US has previously played by. In cases such as terrorism where the value is not in destroying a target but simply in the very act and means of attacking, deterrence may be impossible.[5]

"New Triad"

The 2001 Nuclear Posture Review mandated by Congress was meant for the Department of Defense to determine US nuclear force structure for the coming decade. In recognizing the changing security environment, the DoD used the opportunity in part to establish a blueprint for transforming US strategic posture.[6] Labeled the "New Triad," this strategy shifted from the "one size fits all" nuclear deterrent strategy to a more flexible capability to deter state and non-state actors.[7] While a nuclear capability is still seen to provide a unique and fundamental contribution, the new model offers a combination of new capabilities that went beyond the historic dependence upon nuclear weapons to improve the US' ability to respond to national threats. It recognized that offensive nuclear forces may not be appropriate for deterring the spectrum of potential adversaries the US will face. The New Triad provides a mix of strategic offensive nuclear and non-nuclear strike capabilities; active and passive defenses; and a robust research, development and industrial infrastructure as illustrated in Figure 3.

Figure 3: The Nuclear Triad and the "New Triad"

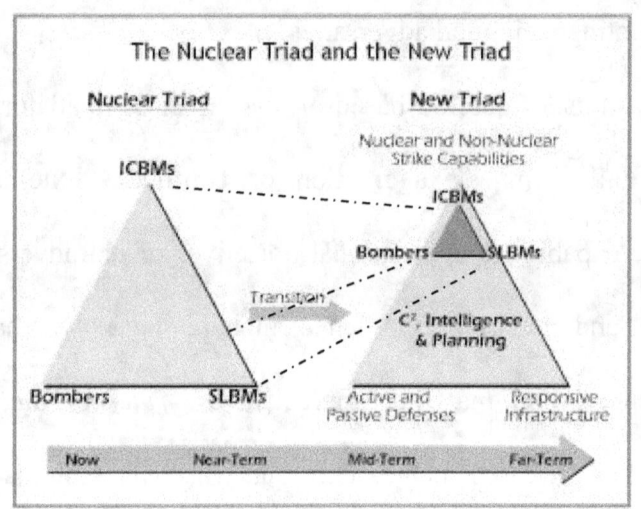

Source: "US Nuclear Stockpile," Office of the Deputy Assistant the the Secretary of Defense for Nuclear Matters, (http://www.acq.osd.mil/ncbdp/nm/images/NewTriad_website.jpg)

This review also argued the US did not have to size or sustain its forces as though Russia was a *smaller version* of its former Cold War self. As a result, the DoD shifted planning of US strategic forces from the traditional threat-based approach to one which was capabilities-based, allowing the military to reduce the number of nuclear weapons while maintaining a credible deterrent.[8]

"Tailored Deterrence"

Just as an offensive nuclear strike capability as a whole is just one *leg* of the New Triad, so the New Triad is just an element within the overall US policy of Tailored Deterrence. Restructuring the deterrent strategy is nothing new. Even throughout the Cold War, questions about the credibility of US nuclear deterrent posture caused the US to *tailor* doctrine, targeting and force structure to ensure adversaries understood the US had both the capacity and the will to respond if attacked.[9] The Bush Administration's focus on tailored deterrence follows the same logic.[10] The Administration's concept may differ from the classic *strategic deterrence* in two ways. First, the strategy seeks to broaden its deterrent audience to include "advanced military competitors, regional WMD states, as well as non-state terrorist networks."[11] Second, the US may be focusing less on deterrent relationships and more on acquiring capabilities to attack and destroy the valued targets of our adversaries since a relationship presumes both sides recognize the consequences of acting.[12] Alternatively, however, "coping with future nuclear threats may require more than just deterrence, and deterrence might need more than just nuclear threats."[13]

The DO-JOC recognizes that the challenges identified in the National Security Strategy require a new concept of capabilities that not only provide for a wider range of military options, but also integrate all elements of national power: diplomatic, informational, military and economic (DIME).[14] The document also argues that "deterrence is most likely effective when the actions and capabilities of the joint force are integrated with those of the interagency and as necessary, non-state and multinational powers."[15] Thus, the most effective deterrent tool may not be a military solution.

Differing adversaries require differing US deterrent means. As expected, each adversary's decision calculus is different since what each adversary values, seeks to gain or fears is unique. Therefore, an effective deterrent strategy must be flexible enough to address both risk-averse and risk-taking adversaries.[16] By adjusting deterrence to fit particular actors, this diverse capacity within the US' *tool kit* allows for a perception by adversaries of a more plausible US response to any broad category of security challenges.

The 2002 National Security Strategy states the "military's highest priority is to defend the United States."[17] Yet to do so effectively, the military must:

- Assure our allies and friends;
- Dissuade future military competition;
- Deter threats against US interests, allies, and friends; and
- Decisively defeat any adversary if deterrence fails.[18]

Strategic deterrence, however, should not be conducted within a vacuum from the other key defense activities as each is integrated in the success of the others.[19] Figure 4 illustrates the impact each activity plays on the others.

Figure 4 Deterrence Impact on Other Key Defense Activities

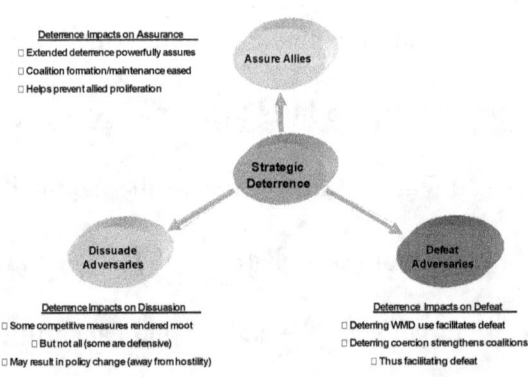

Source: Copied from *Deterrence Operations Joint Operating Concept*, USSTRATCOM, December 2006 (version 2.0), 70.

Although the influence of non-state actors has increased, the international order is still based upon nation-states. Through the cooperation of its allies, the US may effectively shape the choices and subsequently limit the behavior of other actors. This would effectively achieve our objectives.

Exercising decisive influence is the key to effective strategic deterrence. The cause and effect deterrent calculus used between the US and Russia was based upon recognized and understood reasoning driven by limits to technology and shaped by western values. In other words, deterrent strategies were planned and implemented with specific objectives in mind (i.e., deter adversary X from taking action Y under circumstance Z). However, it is unclear whether these perceptions would be equally understood in this new strategic environment. Successful deterrence in the future may rely more on the adversary's perception vice the deterrer's will and capacity.

With respect to a Sino-US deterrent strategy, the key may be a nonmilitary solution. China's strategic tradition emphasizes surprise. Deliberate shows of military force may be misinterpreted, since to the Chinese, an adversary's true intention to use force would have been indicated by discreet preparations.[20] Directly limiting China's freedom of action may be interpreted as a direct threat, causing China to react with a preemptive response. But a strategy of denial by encouraging neighbor states to collectively view her as a rising regional security and economic threat may be the best means to curtailing Chinese objectives.[21] China, and most eastern cultures are communal-based. Merit and success are based upon one's contribution to the larger group, such as family or community. For the neighboring states—as a regional *community*—to collectively reject

33

or exclude China may be the best means to diplomatically manipulate China to its disadvantage.

Deterring rogue states may be more problematic as each has its own motivations and values. There are likely three limited situations in which US deterrent threats against regional adversaries remain credible:

- In response to an adversary's first use of nuclear weapons
- In response to an adversary's use of chemical or biological weapons
- In response to an adversary's threat to overwhelm a major US ground unit, even if the threat is purely conventional.[22]

Because they are likely to maintain a small inventory, it is unlikely they will be a direct threat to the US; however, the concern is their threat within a region where the US offers its extended deterrent umbrella.

Here is where integrated and theater ballistic missile defense may best demonstrate its worth. Currently, most countries view ballistic missiles as the delivery platform of choice. Advertising their ineffectiveness thanks to a reliable defensive system may both dissuade and deter regional threats by negating the adversary's threat. However, this may be a short-term solution since enemies have historically adapted to find alternative means to regain their influence.

In the case of Iran, a *roll back* strategy may offer options. A roll back strategy "involves a series of measures designed to reduce Iranian motivations for retaining its nuclear program along with coercive measures to inflict sufficient punishment on the regime should it not comply."[23] Though it has shown success in curtailing Libya, South Africa, and much of the former Soviet satellite states, the difficulty of its success in Iran is in identifying the proper *carrot and sticks*.[24] However, if Iran does cross the nuclear weapons threshold, a successful roll back effort would be extremely difficult without amplifying both types of motivators.

Effectively deterring North Korea may be more difficult. With respect to its singular goal of maintaining regime survival, it is probably the most rational of countries, and any deterrent strategy will require this tenet to be kept in mind. Similarly with China, effectively deterring regional adversaries will require better understanding of each adversary's motivations. Reassurances with regional allies, strengthening military capabilities and developing defensive ones, and in certain instances, perhaps extending the US deterrent umbrella may be the best means by which the US strengthens its deterrent position.[25]

The greatest challenge facing the US may be effectively deterring terrorism. From a military perspective, "[t]he US may lack critical capabilities required to effectively influence a specific adversary's decision calculations under certain conditions. Because the perceptions and capabilities of potential adversaries vary, the means required to influence them may vary significantly."[26] The best means by which to deter terrorism may have already been stated in the current National Security Strategy: "In leading the campaign against terrorism, we are forging new, productive international relationships and redefining existing ones in ways that meet the challenges of the twenty-first century"[27] and "denying further sponsorship, support, and sanctuary to terrorists by convincing or compelling states to accept their sovereign responsibilities."[28]

The DO-JOC is particularly effective in identifying *how* the US will best achieve deterrence and even outlines a "portfolio approach":

- Credibly threaten to deny [adversaries] the benefits or gains sought
- Credibly threaten to impose costs that are viewed as to painful to incur

- Encourage adversary restraint by convincing the adversary that <u>not</u> undertaking the action we seek to deter will result in an outcome acceptable to him [underscore in original].[29]

But the dilemma is identifying *what* the US can do in this respect to best achieve deterrence.

In all instances, though, the US must maintain its policy of strategic ambiguity. Declaring the conditions that mark the threshold of nuclear weapons use marginalizes any coercive threat. Worse is when the US states "we didn't mean it" after it threatens nuclear weapons use.

Supporting a More Effective Deterrent Model

As recent as the fall of 2008, there have been calls to reexamine the overall US deterrent strategy.[30] The pace and scope of today's challenges demand the US deterrent strategy remains at the pinnacle of effectiveness. Yet short of a revolution in deterrent policy, the current tailored deterrent strategy may be the best means to counter the broad spectrum of US strategic challenges. However, there are three suggestions that may perhaps enhance its effectiveness.

First, the US should remember its leadership role in the international system. The ascendance of China may warrant use of its growing influence as a rising state to shape the international system to its benefit. China may eventually surpass the US as the world's number one economic behemoth; however China or any other emerging nation such as India must realize it must face a Western-centered system that is open, integrated, and rule based giving China greater incentive for integration vice opposition.[31] In a tailored deterrent strategy, effective use of the economic element of national power may help the US to achieve its strategic objectives. By reestablishing itself as the leader of the global system of governance that it has shaped and influenced since the end of World War II, the US will define the environment in which China will make its critical strategic choices.[32]

Second, invest upon the success of DoD's Office of Net Assessment. The DO-JOC states, "Global situational awareness is the foundation of deterrence..." and "[i]mproved understanding of adversary decision-makers' value structures and perceptions...will enhance our ability to tailor deterrence operations."[33] In turn, *net assessment* is defined as:

> The comparative analysis of military, technological, political, economic, and other factors governing the relative military capability of nations. Its purpose is to identify problems and opportunities that deserve the attention of senior defense officials.[34]

An organization that uses the concept of net assessment and cuts across all executive departments can focus its efforts on accurately projecting the influence of all elements of national power against a strategic threat. Among the factors to assess are the adversary's risk-taking propensity and all factors which, in turn, establish the basis of an adversary's decision calculus.

Finally, continue the development and deployment of an effective ballistic missile defense capability. Ballistic missiles currently remain the delivery system of choice and will likely be used to threaten the American homeland or its allies, and restrict US freedom of action within a region. Obviously, this may cause adversary's to seek an alternative method of delivery, but an active defense system will deny the adversary a major part of its own coercive capacity.

A Warning

The US has recognized it was not quick to realize the new challenges facing its national security interests once the Cold War ended; however, it is now aware it can no longer solely rely on a reactive posture.[35] The response has been one of *preemptive* action. Preemptive attack "entails the use of force to quell or mitigate an impending strike by an adversary."[36] While the international community may understand and accept national self defense, the current administration is arguably conducting *preventive* warfare though expressed in the language of preemption. A preventive attack "entails the use of force to eliminate any possible future strike, even when there is no reason to believe that aggression is planned or the capability to launch such an attack is operational."[37] Of concern is how this *Bush Doctrine* may affect the normative order—the international norms and shared values among states—throughout the international community. The fear is not just a reigning hegemon who is promoting a new *code of conduct* but that the frame of reference is altered for everyone else (i.e., what the strongest does, all else will copy).[38] In essence, the US may be promoting exactly what it is attempting to deter. Obviously this may cause somewhat of a credibility gap to the rest of the world.

Notes

[1] Robert M. Gates, Secretary of Defense (*Speech, Carnegie Endowment for International Peace*, Washington DC, 28 Oct 2008).

[2] Buchan, *Future Roles of US Nuclear Forces*, 21.

[3] Department of Defense, *Quadrennial Defense Review Report*, 2006.

[4] Buchan, *Future Roles of US Nuclear Forces*, 101.

[5] Department of Defense, *2008 National Defense Strategy*, 12.

Notes

[6] Nuclear Posture Review Excerpts, submitted to Congress on 31 December 2001, *2001 Nuclear Posture Review*, Forward.

[7] Department of Defense, *2006 Quadrennial Defense Review*, 49.

[8] Nuclear Posture Review Excerpts, submitted to Congress on 31 December 2001, *2001 Nuclear Posture Review*, Forward.

[9] Woolf, *Nuclear Weapons in US National Security Policy,*5.

[10] Ibid.

[11] Ibid., 5-6.

[12] Ibid.

[13] Buchan, *Future Roles of US Nuclear Forces*, 106.

[14] Department of Defense, *Deterrence Operations Joint Operating Concept, v2.0*, December 2006, 3.

[15] Ibid., 9.

[16] Ibid.,, 17.

[17] *2002 National Security Strategy of the United States*, September 2002, 29.

[18] Ibid.

[19] Department of Defense, *Deterrence Operations Joint Operating Concept, v2.0*, December 2006, 70.

[20] Shulsky, *Deterrence Theory and Chinese Behavior*, 53-54.

[21] Ibid., 50.

[22] Watman et al, *US Regional Deterrent Strategies*, 80.

[23] Yaphe & Lutes, *Reassessing Implications of a Nuclear-Armed Iran*, 35.

[24] Ibid.

[25] Ibid., 41.

[26] Department of Defense, *Deterrence Operations Joint Operating Concept, v2.0*, December 2006, 50.

[27] *The National Security Strategy of the United States of America*, September 2002, 7.

[28] Ibid, 6.

[29] Department of Defense, *Deterrence Operations Joint Operating Concept, v2.0*, December 2006, 24.

[30] ADM Michael Mullen, "It's Time For a New Deterrence Model", *Joint Forces Quarterly*, Issue 51 (4th Qtr, 2008): 2-3, http://www.ndu.edu/inss/Press/jfq_pages/i51.html.

[31] G. John Ikenberry, "The Rise of China and the Future of the West", *Foreign Affairs*, Jan/Feb 2008, Vol 87/No1, http://www.foreignaffairs.org/2008/1.html.

[32] Ibid.

[33] Department of Defense, *Deterrence Operations Joint Operating Concept, v2.0*, December 2006, 29.

[34] Department of Defense Directive *(DoDD) 5111.11, Director of Net Assessment,* 22 Aug 2001, certified current as of 23 Apr 2007.

[35] *The National Security Strategy of the United States of America*, September 2002, 15.

Notes

[36] Charles W. Kegley, Jr. & Gregory A. Raymond, "Preventive War and Permissive Normative Order", *International Studies Perspectives*, vol 4 no 4.(Blackwell Publishing, 2003), 388.
[37] Ibid., 385-388.
[38] Ibid., 390-391.

Summary

Nuclear weapons are unmatched as terror weapons and are therefore the most effective possible weapons to implement a policy of deterrence by threat of punishment. This is the most enduring role for nuclear weapons and the one for which they are most uniquely suited.

- Glenn Buchan

Flexibility begets complexity; however the corollary is that complexity, such as that found in the current strategic environment, demands flexibility. The necessity of maintaining a nuclear arsenal is analogous to considering the utility of owning a fire extinguisher in one's home. While there is an investment one makes in purchasing and maintaining a single-purpose, single-use item, the extinguisher provides a peace of mind in its mere presence. The alternative consequence in not having an extinguisher if a fire breaks out is unthinkable. Yet the broad range of threats in today's contemporary world requires the US to have a deterrent strategy that offers greater flexibility than what nuclear weapons can offer. As noted nuclear strategy theorist Glenn Buchan points out,

> Choosing an appropriate role for US nuclear weapons will require balancing potentially competing objectives:
> - Extracting the appropriate value from its nuclear forces (i.e., imposing its will on others in situations where it really matters
> - Making nuclear weapons in general less important rather than more important in world affairs to reduce the incentives for others to acquire them
> - Avoiding operational practices that might appear overly provocative to other nuclear powers and prompt unfortunate responses (e.g. reliance on launch-on-warning or preemption).[1]

Additionally, recent lessons in irregular warfare remind us that the military element of national power will not succeed on its own. In any discussion of United States national security policy, one must remember that strategies, conflicts and wars are not ends unto themselves, but the means by which this country can achieve the goal of preserving and promoting peace, prosperity, security and liberty. But the challenges to these goals from rising or transitioning national powers, rogue states, and transnational aggression are long term and will require emphasis across the entire spectrum of national power.

Notes

[1] Buchan, *Future Roles of US Nuclear Forces*, 114-117.

BIBLIOGRAPHY

Alston, Maj Gen Donald. "The Air Force Nuclear Enterprise." Video teleconference lecture. Air War College, Maxwell AFB, AL, 9 September 2008.

Bracken, Paul. *Fire in the East: The Rise of Asian Military Power and the Second Nuclear Age*. New York, NY: HarperCollins Publishers, 1999.

Brodie, Bernard. *Anatomy of Deterrence*. RAND Report RM-2218. Santa Monica, CA: RAND, July 1958.

Buchan, Glenn et al. *Future Roles of US Nuclear Forces*. RAND Report MR-1231-AF (Santa Monica, CA: RAND Corp, 2003.

Department of Defense Directive (*DoDD*) *5111.11, Director of Net Assessment,* 22 Aug 2001, certified current as of 23 Apr 2007.

Deterrence Operations Joint Operating Concept v2.0, December 2006.

Doughty, Robert, Ira Gruber, Roy Flint, Mark Grimsley, George Herring. *American Military History and the Evolution of Western Warfare*. Boston, MA: Houghton Mifflin, 1996.

Faulconbridge, Guy. "Russia Starts Production of New Ballistic Missiles," *NewsDaily*, 1 Dec 2008 (Reuters), http:\\www.newsdaily.com/stories/tre4b03qa-us-russia-missile/.

Freedman, Lawrence, *Deterrence*. Cambridge: Polity Press, 2004.

Gates, Robert M. Secretary of Defense. "A Balanced Strategy: Reprogramming the Pentagon for a New Age" *Foreign Affairs* 88, no. 1 (January/February 2009): http://www.foreignaffairs.org/20090101faessay88103/robert-m-gates/how-to-reprogram-the-pentagon.html.

Gates, Robert M. Secretary of Defense. Address. Carnegie Endowment for International Peace, Washington DC, 28 October 2008.

George, Alexander. *Forceful Persuasion: Coercive Diplomacy as an Alternative to War*, Washington DC: United States Institute of Peace, 1991.

Ikenberry, G. John, "The Rise of China and the Future of the West." *Foreign Affairs*, Jan/Feb 2008, Vol 87/No1, http://www.foreignaffairs.org/2008/1.html.

Jenkins, Brian M. *Will Terrorists Go Nuclear?* RAND Paper P-5541. Santa Monica, CA: RAND Corp, 1975.

Joint Publication (JP) 1-02, *DoD Dictionary of Military and Associated Terms*, 12 April 2001, (as amended 1 March 2007).

Kegley, Charles W., Jr. & Raymond, Gregory A., "Preventive War and Permissive Normative Order", *International Studies Perspectives*, vol 4 no 4.(Blackwell Publishing, 2003), 388.

Kelly, James A. *Overview of US Policy Toward Taiwan: Testimony at a hearing on Taiwan, House International Relations Committee*, Washington DC, 21 Apr 2004.

Morgan, Patrick M. *Deterrence: A Conceptual Analysis*. 2d ed, Beverly Hills, CA: Sage Publications, 1983.

Mullen, ADM Michael, "It's Time For a New Deterrence Model", *Joint Forces Quarterly*, Issue 51 (4th Qtr, 2008): 2-3, http://www.ndu.edu/inss/Press/jfq_pages/i51.html.

National Defense Strategy, June 2008.

National Security Strategy of the United States of America, 2002, 13.

Njølstad, Olav. "The Development and Proliferation of Nuclear Weapons", *The Norwegian Nobel Institute* (http://nobelprize.org/educational_games/peace/nuclear_weapons/readmore.html).

Nuclear Posture Review (Excerpts), submitted to Congress on 31 December 2001, *2001 Nuclear Posture Review Report*.

Ochmanek, David & Schwartz, Lowell H. *Challenge of Nuclear Armed Regional Adversaries*. Santa Monica, CA: RAND Corp, 2008.

Paal, Douglas and Tucker, Dr. Nancy Bernkopf. Interview by Andrea Koppel. "China and Taiwan: An American Tightrope." *Transcript of Great Decisions TV 2001*, (http://www.fpa.org/topics_info2414/topics_info_show.htm?doc_id=77090).

Pape, Robert A. *Bombing to Win: Air Power and Coercion in War*. Ithaca, NY: Cornell University Press, 1996.

Scobell, Andrew. *North Korea's Strategic Intentions*. Carlisle Barracks, PA: Strategic Studies Institute, US Army War College, 2005.

Sheikh, Fawzia. "Pentagon Lays Out Three Obstacles to Nuclear Deterrence—Space Challenge Also Cited." *Inside the Pentagon*. 17 July 2008.

Shulsky, Abram M. *Deterrence Theory and Chinese Behavior*. RAND Report MR-1161-AF. Santa Monica, CA: RAND Corp, 2000.

The American Heritage® Dictionary of the English Language, Fourth Edition. "deter", Houghton Mifflin Company, 2004. http://dictionary.reference.com/browse/deter.

Watman, Kenneth, Wilkening, Dean, Arquilla, John, and Nichiporuk, Brian. *US Regional Deterrence Strategies*. RAND Report MR-490-A/AF Santa Monica CA: RAND Corp, 1995.

Wilkening, Dean & Watman, Kenneth. *Nuclear Deterrence in a Regional Context*. RAND Report MR-500-A/AF. Santa Monica, CA: RAND Corp, 1995.

Woolf, Amy F. *Nuclear Weapons in US National Security Policy: Past, Present, and Prospects*. CRS Report RL34226. Washington DC: Congressional Research Service, updated January 2008.

Yaphe, Judith S. and Lutes, Charles D. *Reassessing the Implications of a Nuclear-Armed Iran*. McNair Paper 69. Washington, DC: Institute for National Strategic Studies, NDU, 2005.